Fancy Running?

The How to Guide to Fancy Dress Marathon Running

"Adversity causes some men to break; others to break records."

William Arthur Ward

Philip J Rose

Published in the United Kingdom by Malabar Publishing

Cover and Book design by Matt Wright, Nobleword

ISBN 978-1-9163527-0-4 (paperback)

ISBN 978-1-9163527-1-1 (eBook)

My special thanks to Matt Wright of Nobleword, for his help
in getting this book finished and the cover designed.

Dedicated to my loving (and very understanding) wife, Claire,
for all her support over my years and years of running,
especially during these last five years whilst I've combined
running with dressing up to raise a bit more money for good
causes. Also thank you to my beautiful daughters who don't
(yet) have the fancy dress running bug, but already recognise
the benefit of keeping fit.

Thank you to all those people who donated so generously to
keep me running and raising much needed funds for the
charities I chose to support.

And finally, to Alan and Angela, my mum and dad, who gave
me the desire to keep myself fit and helped create my two
biggest costumes. Without your hard work and sewing skills
'Little Miss Sunshine' and 'The Sun'
wouldn't have made it to the start line, let alone win a
Guinness World Record!

Contents

Chapter 1.   So, you've decided to run your first marathon in fancy dress… you fool!

> *"Run when you can, walk if you have to, crawl if you must; just never give up."*
>
> **Dean Karnazes**

Oh no, you've decided to take the plunge and sign up for your first marathon in fancy dress. Good on you. You are joining a group of committed (some might say foolish) people who take on this challenge each year for fun.

Looking back, I realise I've been a 'closet' fancy dress runner for years. It all started when I ran my first London marathon in 2008. I realised in my training runs that there were lots of people in the race and everyone looked the same, give or take. As a spectator it was a tough job to spot 'your runner', so, I needed to find a way of standing out… and being only slight extroverted at the time, my

fancy dress of choice was… a blue wig. Ok, I know it wasn't a full fancy dress outfit, but running a marathon was hard enough in those days without donning the full costume!

As time went by, I became better at running and more
confident. I entered more half-marathons and marathons and
realised I was:

- Good at running

- Keen to raise more money for charity

- Needing another challenge (as if running a
  marathon wasn't hard enough!)

- Slightly mad?

Now, you and I both know that you don't have to be mad to
dress up, but you do need a sense of humour, because you
will get laughed at. Your children, partner, parents and even
your pets will think you are a little bit bonkers. And that's
where the fun comes from.

So, I'm guessing that, as you've downloaded / bought / been
given / stolen this book, you did so for a reason… and that's
probably because you want to improve your chances of
surviving your first fancy dress marathon. In which case,
welcome to the slightly quirky but amazing family of fancy
dress runners!

And remember, as they say, once you've done it in fancy
dress, you'll never ever go back… life will never be the same!

Top Tips – Taking the first steps

1. First things first – you need to get the dates in your diary early if you want to enter the big races like the London Marathon.
2. Secondly, once you know the entry dates, remember to check the race requirements, specifically to find out if fancy dress is permitted and whether there are any restrictions (i.e. regarding size…etc).
3. It goes without saying (in most cases) to remember that your entry is in on time — no entry, no race!

Chapter 2.   Signing up - Committing to unleashing your Inner Hero!

> *"I don't run to add days to my life, I run to add life to my days."*
>
> **Ronald Rook**

Once you've committed yourself mentally to the challenge (and it is mental as well as physical), you will need to find a race (if you haven't already done so already) that accepts fancy dress. The reason I say this, is that some races are for so-called 'serious runners'. I have run a number of races in the past in my traditional running gear where I received the distinct impression that fancy dress would not have been welcomed!

The funny thing is, I actually quite like turning up in my 'fancy dress' and then beating half of the more serious runners … that's probably why it's frowned upon!

Some of the big races certainly do welcome fancy dress, although most have guidelines as to what is acceptable, mainly on the grounds of safety.

In my view, the most fun marathon to do is London. I say 'fun' in all seriousness as I think this is the most 'fun' run you will ever do in your life. The smiles of the crowds along the whole of the 26.2 miles are nothing but awe-inspiring. I have run London five times to date and have loved it every time. There is no better feeling than bringing your fancy dress costume to London (something we'll discuss later in this book).

I would always recommend knowing that you can complete a race without the additional burden of fancy dress — trust me, it will make it harder for you! If you do have your sights set on running in fancy dress, be sure to schedule other smaller or shorter races / events that you can enter beforehand. This will give you the confidence to know that you can do it and will also provide you with a feel for how different races work (and whether they accept fancy dress runners!)

Top Tips – Signing Up

4. Many people choose to run in fancy dress either to raise more money or to increase their profile. If that's you, then good luck! However, be aware of the additional load this will put on (a) your training time, (b) your body, and (c) your mental state, both in training and before the race.
5. Check on the specific rules and stipulations for your chosen record attempt (more about that later).
6. Be persistent and confident in your determination to succeed in completing your chosen race.

Chapter 3.   Creating your Costume

*"We all have dreams, in order
to make dreams come into
reality, it takes an awful lot of
determination, dedication,
self-discipline and effort."*

Jesse Owens

Once you have pencilled your race in the diary and have it in
mind to run in fancy dress, the next thing is to sort out the
costume.

This can be as easy or challenging as you wish, although in
my view, the more challenging the better! When I last ran
London in fancy dress in 2019, I chose a very large costume
that required a great deal of time, patience and effort to get
right. However, bear in mind that I was already an
experienced runner and had run previous shorter races in
some form of fancy dress so knew it was possible in principle.

The key to your success as a fancy dress runner is working out
your reason for doing it. Before you commit to a costume,
you need to think why you are dressing up in the first place –
is it to make a statement; to make the run more difficult (ha
ha!); to satisfy your inner show-off or simply to raise your
profile so you can raise more money? Some people (like me,
when I ran my first 'London' in 2008), will just choose a
fancy wig, some will opt for a tutu, some will be content with

fancy leggings… while others will go for something a little more extreme.

For me, one of the biggest reasons behind wanting to dress up to run was simply to improve awareness of my chosen charity and therefore, to raise more money for my cause.

It is vital to decide early on what you want to wear and why. For most people, it comes down to six reasons (or seven, if you include downright stupidity):

- Raise awareness for a charity or good cause

- Raise more money for your charity

- Have more fun than just running in a vest and shorts

- Show off

- Stand out for your supporters

- Or… to get in the Guinness Book of Records.

Ok, so I said six reasons, but having thought about it there are probably quite a few more. The trick is, in my opinion, to do it for the fun of it, even if it might not look like fun to your family and friends.

3.1   Suggestions for costumes

One of the biggest questions I often get asked is… what costume should I wear? My answer is always… it depends.

It depends upon how big an impact you want to create and how much you want to stand out. Here is my list of examples from people I have met at various marathons and events. I have listed these in order of 'Least Conspicuous to Most Conspicuous'. I say 'conspicuous', because running in fancy dress really is to me about standing out. You have to be prepared for people to stop, look and stare. They'll wonder what the heck you are and what you are doing… and that's the fun part of it.

Running in costume is a great way
to meet people!

Least "Conspicuous"	A wig (2008) Bright leggings A Tutu A brightly coloured tutu (2010)
Medium "Conspicuous"	Superman / woman / hero Hulk Captain America A mummy A scout / guide / nurse uniform A wedding dress
Most "Conspicuous"	Little Miss Sunshine (2018) The Sun (2019) Mr Tickle A giant doll A unicorn A tent A giant panda A rhino An elephant

Costume choice depends on how much you are
willing to stand out!

TOP TIPS – Costume Choice

7. Decide why you want to run in costume. Is it to raise more money for your chosen charity? Is it to raise awareness of a particular cause? Is it to break a record? Or is it all of the above?
8. Decide how much impact you want your costume to have; i.e. how much do you really want to stand out?
9. Ask yourself how physically and mentally fit you are? Running in a big costume will take a lot of effort and willpower.
10. If running for a record attempt, consider the impact that weight, size, and aerodynamics will have on your chances.
11. Do some research for inspiration — consider looking through gallery photos from previous marathons and events.
12. Are you planning on running on your own or as a team? If in a team, how many of you will be involved i.e. 2-person costumes, or multi-person?

Chapter 4.   Training your inner Superhero

"If you fail to prepare, you're prepared to fail."

Mark Spitz

It is hard enough merely to train for a 'normal' marathon or race and so training to run one in fancy dress is a far bigger challenge as any costume will increase your weight and hinder your pace. Having said that, in my opinion, in all of my marathon training programmes, specific training is by far the biggest single thing, alongside nutrition, that you need to consider for any marathon or long run.

My marathon training programmes normally last for around 16 weeks[1] and the same goes for fancy dress running. The difference is that whilst I am still developing the costumer, I make sure that I do some of my early runs wearing a rucksack filled with extra weights. For my recent marathons in 2018 and 2019, I filled my rucksack with a couple of ankle weights (because they were soft) and then progressively filled my water pack as my training progressed.

I also include other types of training in my fancy dress training schedule, such as weight training to condition my body for the extra costume load, Pilates to strengthen my core, and swimming to take the pressure off my legs. This cross-training

---

[1] I often use one of the Garmin training plans from Garmin connect

was essential over past couple of years for two reasons: (1) I was getting older and needed more core strength, and (2) my back ached from carrying the costume which bounced awkwardly as I ran.

My weekly schedule typically looks like this:

Sunday	Long Run
Monday	Early morning Swim Evening Pilates
Tuesday	Circuit Training Recovery Run
Wednesday	Weight training
Thursday	Interval Run Circuit training
Friday	Recovery Run or rest day
Saturday	Parkrun or fartlek or hills

I know this looks a lot written down and I do understand why my family gets a little bit annoyed with all my training. So, by all means adapt a training plan that suits you based on your current level of fitness, the time you have available for training and your own life/work balance needs. I include additional cross-training, such as weight training, and Pilates, because I enjoyed these activities and they helped build my core strength which supported my back throughout my training and the final race. The essential training elements I recommend for a costumed runner are:

(1)   A long run
(2)   A recovery run
(3)   Interval runs
(4)   Some form of cross-training to suit your schedule

Now remember, I'm not a personal trainer or running coach so this is purely based upon my own experience. If you're unsure, please find someone who's got a qualification and is able to give you more professional advice. For example, I suggest you check out George Anderson at Intelligent Running[2].

> **TOP TIPS – Training and Advice**
>
> 13. Plan your training schedule well in advance of your chosen event. (e.g. most experts recommend around 16 weeks for a marathon).
> 14. Find a training plan that works for you and then train in your costume regularly to get used to it.
> 15. If you feel you need expert advice, check out George Anderson at Intelligent Running.
> 16. Include training runs in your costume early on — this will help you to 'iron out' any issues before they become a real problem.

---

[2] [2] George Anderson
https://bygeorgeanderson.com/online/#running

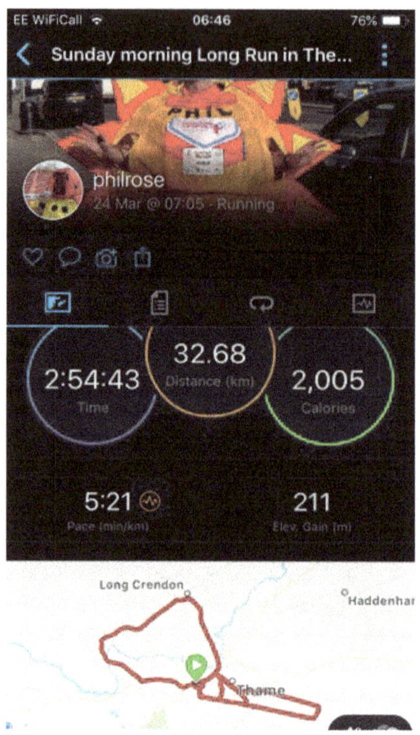

Long Runs are an essential part of your marathon training plan – in costume!

Chapter 5.   Mindset and willpower

"I run because if I didn't, I'd be sluggish and glum and spend too much time on the couch. I run to breathe the fresh air. I run to explore. I run to escape the ordinary. I run...to savor the trip along the way. Life becomes a little more vibrant, a little more intense. I like that."

Dean Karnazes

Without willpower and a "I can do this" mindset, you are likely to fail!

However, willpower and mindset alone will only be effective once you have a goal to direct your mind towards! A quick search online about the subject of goal setting will throw up many results from books and online articles. The reason being that goal setting is essential to achieving anything in life. That includes completing a marathon in fancy dress (or simply completing a marathon for many runners). Writing down your goals is key as this makes it 'real'. Once you have made your intention clear, it's amazing what your mind will do to get it done!

In goal setting, people often talk about setting SMART goals. That means to make your goal:

*S*pecific – "I want to complete the London Marathon in 2020."

*M*easurable – "I want to complete the London Marathon in a superhero costume in 3 hours and 52 minutes."

*A*chievable – It is truly possible for me to do this! It may be stretching to achieve my goal, but it is possible for *me!*

*R*elevant – achieving my goal matters to me and it aligns with where I am in my life. It will help me to raise money, to keep fit, and I see it as worthwhile.

*T*imebound – the race is on 26th April 2019. I know that date and can put a training plan in place between 1st January and race day.

In setting a goal like this and committing it to paper (in a logbook or journal), you are saying to yourself, "I can do this; I have a plan and can make it work!" That's a big part of the first step and will help you as you go through the inevitable ups and downs of your training over the months ahead.

Another key to success is your own willpower and in particular, what you say to yourself.

I'm a big believer in positive mental self-talk, having practiced it for years (I say 'mental' self-talk as last time I tried talking to myself out loud on a crowded train, I received a few weird looks!)

Whenever I am planning to run, or whenever I am running, I have conversations with myself in my head. The conversation before I start my run (usually when I am lying in bed in the dark just before my alarm goes off) goes something like this:

"It's nice and warm in here and dark outside…
maybe I'll just stay here for another few minutes…"

"No, I will feel better in myself if I get up and run as planned."

"A few more minutes here in the warm won't hurt…"

"You will feel so much more positive if you get out of bed NOW!"

"Just lay here… no one knows you planned to run today so no one will be on your back…"

"Be quiet, remember why you are doing this. You chose to do this so you could be fit and enjoy race day."

"No one will know!"

"I will know! And now I remember why I'm doing this!"

With that, I usually jump out of bed, put my kit on[3] under the light of my head torch, and head straight out of the door... (but not always!!!)

Now, I know this all takes will power so I always make sure I am clear on WHY I am doing my running. When I am clear on that I can always (well most of the time) defeat that nagging negative voice in my head.

My 'why' (whilst we are talking about it) is "To Inspire" — that guides everything that I do. Knowing my 'why' makes my training runs even more important as I want to inspire more people every day. I know that by doing my training I will inspire my own confidence. I know that I will be able to run the distance and I know that, on race day when the crowds are shouting my name, I might inspire another person to go out and run a marathon (or just run) and raise money for a good cause!

An additional training hack (to make it easier to get out of bed and run) is to always ensure that your running kit, shoes and food / drinks are ready and laid out the night before. That way you will have nothing to distract you before your run in the morning. If you prefer to run at different times of the day (or you *have* to run at different times) then I would still recommend getting your gear ready early, so it's there when you need it! It will make your decision to train easier as it's one less thing that could 'stop' you getting out the door.

5.1   Keep a log

Many people keep diaries or journals about their life in general. For me, this is an essential piece of training kit for the mindset challenge. Here's a diary excerpt from my 2018 campaign:

> "It's been a tough week since my half marathon last Sunday - not least because of the cold and the snow! After my first half-marathon training run in costume last week I had pain in my toes and my right knee. The physio told me to stop running last week in preparation for a 20-mile run next week in Bedford (March 25th). I've been swimming and using the X Trainer instead, but now want to get out and run again…hoping the pain won't come back!"

The great thing about keeping a diary is you can reflect to yourself on your progress, 'warts and all', and can then see the impact that your training is having on your mental and physical fitness over time.

Here's another entry from the later on that year, showing how my spirits had obviously improved…

> "The last week has been great - everything is going well (touch wood!) I ran the Bedford 20 Mile race on Sunday in Costume in 3 hours and felt pretty good at the end. The next few days my legs were a little stiff - but nothing too bad! So, all the training is coming together."

Your diary doesn't have to be anything too fancy; a simple notebook and pen will do or, if you want to be more

sophisticated, you can use an online site like Garmin
Connect[4] to record all the details, including your log.

Top tips – Mindset

17. Remember WHY you are doing this!
18. Set your SMART goals to guide your mind to help
    you achieve your aim
19. Keeping a log of your runs, both in and out of
    costume is an essential part of any running journey.
20. Logbooks help you realise how far you've come, and;
21. Logbooks are amazing to look back on at the end of
    your journey and realise what a hero you really are!
22. For my logbook I am now totally digital, having used
    Garmin Connect for some years. It's easy to fill in and
    connects automatically to my Garmin Forerunner 935
    (other watches and online tools are available, but I
    haven't had any experience of them.)

---

[4] https://connect.garmin.com/

Chapter 6.   Pain

"Pain is inevitable. Suffering
is optional."

Haruki Murakami

I mention pain in this section, as I know that at some stage in your training, things will begin to hurt. It's inevitable (or maybe that's just me?)

Every marathon runner I know of, at some stage suffers from any number of problems with their legs, back, neck, arms, feet, etc... These injuries will often impact your training and so it's how you manage and deal with them that makes the difference. When I ran my first marathon, I was practically an inpatient with my local chiropractor, Juliet. I also had a standing order[5] for a sports massage!

However, running in costume will throw up extra problems to deal with. During my last two fancy dress marathons, I had issues with the costume rubbing on different parts of my body as I ran. As I became more tired, that rubbing started to hurt a lot more especially with the addition of sweat and rain into the mix.

There are various ways of managing and dealing with the pain of marathon running. However, for me the key is preparation and body conditioning. By body conditioning I mean alternatives to pure cardio work, activities such as Pilates,

---

[5] Ok, so I exaggerate – I didn't have a standing order, but I did see Andrea virtually every other week, which was painful at the time but oh so good later!

yoga, or swimming are great strengtheners that help all runners, including fancy dressers!

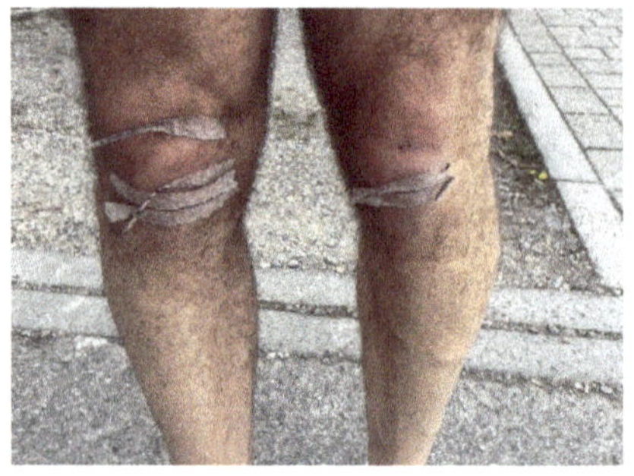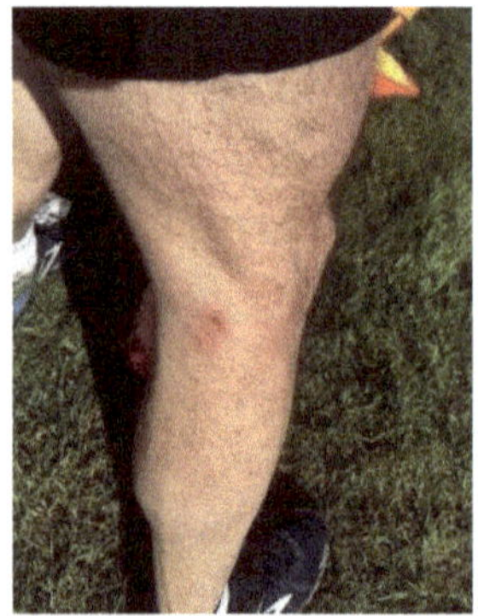

My knees after a training run! – even the back of my leg was painful…

During preparation for London in 2019, I ran the Hampton Court Half Marathon in costume as practice. I didn't realise at the time that the new costume sat lower on my shoulders and also rubbed my knee differently as I ran.

The result was that after 100 minutes of running, I developed a completely numb right kneecap that lasted for a week. The adrenaline of the day got me through the race, but the subsequent numb knee was something I had not experienced before. However, what it did was teach me to adjust the costume to take away some of the bounce and to tape my knees with KT Tape to prevent any further rubbing. At first, I found that the KT Tape didn't stick very well, so I had to shave my knees the day before the race… which was quite a strange experience!

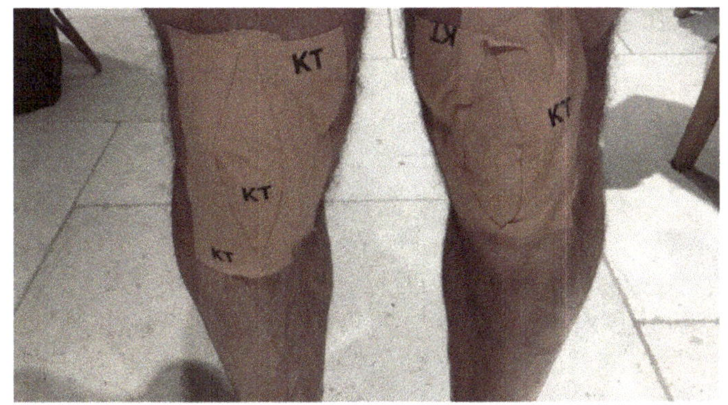

After shaving my knees, I found KT Tape worked
wonders to stop chaffing…!

TOP TIPS – *Costume running injury and pain*

23. Practice in your costume well in advance of your main race.
24. Experiment with different configurations of your costume.
25. Listen to your body to pinpoint pain points.
26. Take up Pilates to strengthen your core.
27. Learn to manage the pain!
28. Listen to your inner voices and be mindful of the positive and negative self-talk.

6.1   Massage and physio

Just a short note on this to say that I think sports massage is an absolutely essential part of my training. During my heavy training periods, I foam roll my legs most days and find that having a good massage really gets my legs and back sorted. In my opinion, even though it might be regarded as an expensive luxury, I would book a sports massage in at least every three weeks and more frequently in the last three weeks before the big day.

As I mentioned earlier, running a marathon in a costume adds a lot of extra pressure to parts of your body that probably never concerned you before. The problem with most large costumes is the fact they bounce at a different rate to your running steps. This means that as your body goes up the costume is often coming down, either on your shoulders, your arms, or your hips. Every bounce adds an extra load so that at the end of every race, you will notice a few different pains.

So, my advice is simple… if you ache, get it sorted quickly, otherwise it will hinder you as you progress further with your training. I have used the services of both a local physiotherapist and a chiropractor at various times and would now swear by their experience to get me to the start line!

Chapter 7.   Sponsorship

> *"Make sure your worst enemy*
> *doesn't live between your own*
> *two ears."*
>
> **Laird Hamilton**

One of the main reasons most people dress up for a run (apart from the fact they just love dressing up!) is that it is a great way to generate sponsorship for charity. Since 2008, I have raised money for charities that meant something to me. The trouble was, that after the first few times of asking for sponsorship, your friends and family start to try to avoid you because they know you're just going to ask them for more money. That was one of the key reasons I chose to start dressing up!!!

There are many things you can do to raise awareness for your chosen cause; I find that the bigger the fancy dress, the bigger the challenge and ultimately, the bigger the reward!

To help me generate sponsorship, here's a list of the things I have done that you could also try:

- Send a letter / email to all your friends, colleagues and family asking for money
- Set up a donation page. I have used JustGiving and Virgin Giving in the past and both work equally well. (Note: You may want to check the fees that each charge for the service before making your choice)

- Send regular emails updates about your training
- Social media: where would we be without social media to help drive awareness of our efforts? It's the one time of the year I consistently use Facebook and Instagram in order to shamelessly promote my cause. You can check out some of my Instagram posts at https://www.instagram.com/phil_runs_uk (more about this later),
- Letters to companies you know, both locally and further afield. This has worked well for me for every charity run I've ever done. Be selective and send a letter to the Managing Director or owner. It's amazing how generous some companies can be!
- Advertising on your costume as you run: people event stopped me in the street to give me cash!

Sometimes the best sponsorship isn't always in financial terms (thank you Nakd!)

7.1   Self-Promotion

It goes without saying, I hope, that the key to sponsorship is self-promotion. If you want to raise money, then there is no use hiding away if you are planning on running in fancy dress. You are probably already someone who doesn't mind people staring as you run by! So, make the most of the opportunities that exist for your own self-promotion in order to raise awareness of what you are doing and who you are doing it for.

Here are my top tips for getting yourself and your cause out there:

1. Contact local newspapers and online news services – they are always interested in local stories.
2. National press: if you really want your name out there!
3. Local radio stations: these are a great opportunity for you, if you don't mind speaking to a presenter either down the line or face-to-face. It's good fun. but for some it can be a little daunting.
4. Local TV: as with local radio, this can be great fun if not a little daunting at first.

Shamelessly promote your charity wherever you go!

Local Radio provides a great opportunity for the fancy dress runner (ha ha)!

Here's an example of a press release I wrote to generate sponsorship and to promote awareness of the cause I was running for in 2018.

Why I'm running the marathon again to beat a World Record and raise vital funds for Children with Cancer.

Philip Rose is planning to do what many people consider unthinkable, and some even say downright silly. This year he is training to become the fastest Little Miss Sunshine in London on April 22nd! That day he is running the London Marathon to raise money for Children with Cancer UK and decided to do something a little different from the start. "I have run the London marathon three times previously," says Philip. "So decided this year I needed to do something a little different if I was to raise £2500 in 4 months."

"My challenge, which many people have told me is totally mad, is to run the marathon dressed as 'Little Miss Sunshine'."

Over the next three months you will probably see Philip out running most days around Long Crendon and Thame – sometimes incognito and at other times disguised as Little Miss Sunshine! If you do see him, please shout hello!

To donate to Children with Cancer UK go to
https://uk.virginmoneygiving.com/PhilRoseVLM2018

For businesses there are opportunities for corporate sponsorship… you can claim a promotional 'space' on Little Miss Sunshine's body during training – please give Phil a call on 0771 283 1775 or drop him an email to philsmarathon@outlook.com

A little about Children with Cancer UK. (https://www.childrenwithcancer.org.uk)

Almost 4,000 children and young people are diagnosed with cancer every year in the UK. That's ten every day. Children with Cancer UK is the leading national children's charity dedicated to the fight against childhood cancer. Our aims are to determine the causes, find cures and provide care for children with cancer. – ENDS

Running in fancy dress requires a particular sense of humour and the total absence of fear of publicity. It's actually great to see your name in print, in all sorts of publications:

7.2   Social Media

I won't say too much more about the benefits of social media here as there are many, many resources out there that will help you with your social media presence. All I will say though is… be prepared to use all the channels you can to promote your cause. The more exposure you can get, the more your chosen charity will benefit.

So, instead of teaching you more here I thought I would just show your some of my favourite social media posts[6]…

Chapter 8. Practise, Practise, Practise

**"The miracle isn't that I
finished. The miracle is that I
had the courage to start."**

John Bingham

Race day preparation is critical for success. As they say in the
armed forces: "Proper Planning Prevents Poor Performance".
You will need to practice running long distances in your
costume, and as mentioned in section 0 you will (probably)
experience some form of pain and anxiety during your
training. Proper planning and preparation will help to manage
or minimise those feelings on race day.

As with any race you will (probably) be nervous on the day so
getting your kit ready beforehand is essential

Every[7] marathon runner knows the 'joy' of carb loading!

I recommend doing at least the last three long runs in full costume, unaided. By unaided, I mean being self-sufficient with water and food as if for the race. This acts as your full race prep. As part of my last marathon training plan, I ran three 30K runs on consecutive Sundays in my costume. These runs were simply 10 km loops around Thame where I live. I chose this because I knew I could park my car close to my run route and would pass that point every 10 km, just in case I needed to make alterations to the costume.

---

[7] Actually, that's not exactly true as I know there is a movement now for some runners to run "Low Carb High Fat" (LCHF).

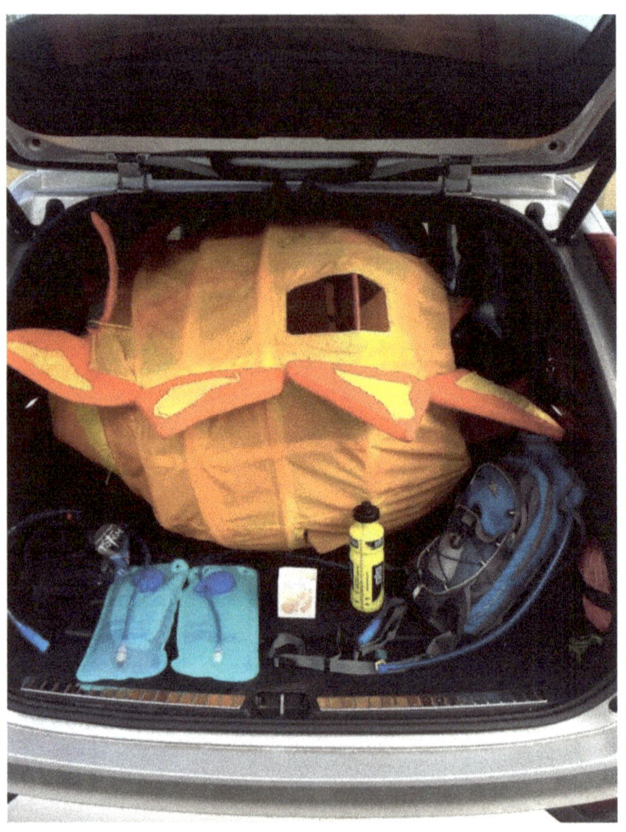

Preparing for your long runs takes time but is well worth it!

The other major benefit of doing my 10 km loops was that people saw me out and about. This did two things for me: first, it boosted my motivation because people always smiled or said hello (or simply laughed at me) and secondly, it gave me more exposure for fundraising (more of that later). It was during one of these runs that I decided to print off some tear-off sponsorship address tabs that I could hand out to people if they asked why I was running. This generated a good few extra donations from some very kind people.

On these long runs I made sure I carried the same nutrition I intended to eat on race day. You will read in many race plans about the importance of nutrition and specifically trying it out BEFORE the big day. There is no point arriving at the race and starting to worry about how your nutrition will work if you haven't tried it beforehand. I've seen too many people struggle throughout their big race because of a lack of nutrition prep. My costume for London 2019 was very big. This meant I couldn't easily get my hands to my mouth to eat or drink. My solution was to sew a small food pouch into the inside of the costume that held my gels for the race and to carry a small water bladder in a rucksack so that I could always drink and eat on the run.

Food pockets sewn into the inside of the costume saved the day!

In the 2018 London Marathon, I had arranged for my ever-supportive wife to be at mile 10 with an additional bottle of electrolyte fluid. I had learned that I needed to continually monitor my levels of dehydration throughout my running and knew I needed to refill my backpack at some point. So, having Claire on the course with my refill meant she could simply pour the liquid into my backpack bladder without me having to remove or adjust the costume. I only learned this from my practice runs.

The other key thing I learned from my practices, and from my previous marathon experience, was my need for salt at around 17 miles. In 2018, I had to ask a child on the pavement for one of their crisps! So, in 2019 I taped a pack of salt and vinegar crisps to the inside of the costume 'just in case of emergency'. Again, this was a learning point from my training.

Proper preparation before a race takes planning
(with a little help from the dog!)

29. Remember the 5 Ps of success: "Proper Planning Prevents Poor Performance", or put more positively… "Proper Planning and PRACTICE ensures Perfect Performance"

Chapter 9.   Race Day

"If you are losing faith in human nature, go out and watch a marathon."

Kathrine Switzer

This is it. This is what you've been training for! All your preparation has come down to this one day. So, get it right! I say, "Get it right!" to look at the positive intent rather than saying "Don't @"C! it up!" Remember, your brain gives you what you ask it, so be mindful of what you ask for in the first place.

Most marathons I have run start early in the morning, so you will need to prepare for early morning running during your pre-race prep and training. Even if the start time appears reasonable, you will need to be there well before you are due to run, especially if you are in costume. The London Marathon used to start at 9:30am when I first ran it, but has since been changed to 9:45am, and with the introduction of different start waves, your own start could be even later. However, most runners like to arrive early to allow them to prepare and to enjoy the pre-race atmosphere – which is an even better experience if you are in fancy dress.

Remember, getting to the start takes some planning. You will probably either need to book a hotel close to the start or arrange transport to get yourself and your costume there.

Consideration needs to be given early on to how you will transport your costume!

I always go by bus with a local running club. It's an early 5:30am start but it takes the hassle out of it for me and is one less thing to worry about[8].

---

[8] Or at least it should be one less thing to worry about! In 2019 it actually added to my pre-race nerves. First the bus was late arriving at the pickup point and then had to stop en-route to change the driver's tacho. Then, as we got close to London the bus driver got lost! In the end I had to grab my phone and navigate the 53-seat bus through the streets to the drop-off point. For 'normal' runners this wouldn't be a problem, but I was a little nervous as I had to be at

9.1   Race day nutrition

Tim Noakes

Appropriate nutrition on race day is essential, so it's worth
planning what and when you will eat and drink as you head
to the start line. Breakfast at 5:30am isn't easy for most of us,
so make sure you have a plan of what you want to eat and
have practiced with it beforehand.

My ideal race day breakfast is a bowl of overnight oats made
with chia seeds, raisins, protein powder, ground pumpkin and
sunflower seeds mixed with oat or almond milk. I make this
the night before, leaving it to soak in the fridge.

I also take a toasted bagel with peanut butter and jam to eat
on the coach along with a mug of green tea.

In my race bag I carry a 500ml bottle of energy drink and a
bottle of water to ensure I am hydrated. Currently I prefer SIS
energy drinks as I have trained with them for years but, once
again, make your own choice based on what works best for
you.

---

the start early for my official adjudication by Guinness World
Records.

Once you are at the start of the race you can really relax and enjoy the pre-race atmosphere. I've been lucky that the weather has been great for each of the marathons I have run in fancy dress – although 2018 was the hottest London Marathon on record!

9.2   Toilets

I only include this bit here for a bit of fun… and to make you aware of it. Toilets are a running issue (excuse the pun) for all runners and being in costume adds an extra layer of complexity to that. All runners know they need to hydrate and so the issue becomes how to get rid of the excess. Factor in pre-race nerves AND a costume and it becomes even more fun!

So, I would urge you to prepare for this element of the race in the same way as you approached your nutrition. There's no point in turning up at the start, needing a wee and then being unable to get out of your costume, or worse still, as was the case for me, being too big to get in the cubicle in the first place!

I know this might be more than you want to think about right now, but believe me, it's important if you don't want to be too embarrassed!

9.3   The crowds

All I can say here is enjoy the crowd. If you've got your prep right, then today is your day. As a fancy dress runner, you will certainly receive a big cheer from the crowd. This is the part that really drives me on. I love the noise and the excitement

of people shouting my name (always write your name on
your running vest or costume if you want to get noticed and
receive that extra bit of encouragement). I also love the smiles
that running in costume brings to everyone you pass on the
way, especially the kids on the street. So, take your time and
play to the crowd; after all, this is your 15 minutes of fame (or
4 hours plus if you're running a marathon!)

9.4   Pacing

As with any race whether you are in running kit or costume,
remember to stick to your race plan. There are no prizes for
not finishing because you got carried away with the
excitement of your race. Remember that you are in costume
and so your race pace will most probably (depending on your
costume) be slower than your normal pace. You will have
trained for a certain pace, so now you need to stick to it. If
you do, you will finish. Enough said!

9.5   The unexpected

As with many things in life, marathon runners (and especially
fancy dress marathon runners) need to be prepared for the
unexpected… especially on or before race day. It is important
to be aware of the temperature and weather in general. Races
(normally) happen whatever the weather[9], so you need to be
prepared for anything and everything.

---

[9] Actually, one of my training half marathons in 2018 was cancelled
because of snow, as was the Oxford Santa Run 2017.

For example, the 2018 London Marathon was the hottest on record. This made it especially uncomfortable for the runners wearing enormous costumes… like me.

The key was a combination of moderating my pace – I had planned to run 4 hours that day and ended up running 4 hours 26 minutes – and managing your mindset through the race.

All marathon runners need to listen to their bodies and respond accordingly. It's no use ploughing on ignoring vital signs – especially dehydration. This is IMPORTANT. You MUST manage your water and salt intake accordingly to ensure the successful completion of your race. If it's hot, be mindful of how much water you drink and how much electrolyte you take in.

2018

2019

30. Enjoy your race day – it's what you have been training for!
31. Hydrate properly! Please seek advice and guidance on this as it is key to your success and safety, e.g. the London Marathon website has specific information on hydration for 'normal' runners. However, remember you will most probably sweat more in your costume so will need more fluid and electrolyte on a long run.
32. Manage your energy – eat appropriate food before the race and top up your energy as you run.
33. Stick to your pace.
34. Don't try anything new on race day – if you haven't done it before in training, don't do it today!
35. Work the crowds. They will love seeing you in your costume and you'll get a buzz from the noise they make!

Chapter 10. Post Race

"Some of the world's greatest feats were accomplished by people not smart enough to know they were impossible."

Doug Larson

Congratulations. You've done it!

You can relax. Well almost – first please make sure you stretch those muscles. If you've run a marathon before you know how important this is AND how difficult it can also be. The costume will make it even more tricky, and once you reach the end, you'll probably have a little way to walk before you pick up your bag and recovery drinks and meet your supporters. The energy and emotion of the event may well overtake you – it always gets to me when I finish. I remember once finishing the London Marathon and starting to cry tears of joy as I lifted my leg for the volunteer to take my timing chip off my shoe. She looked at me and said, "you can't cry now it's all over!" To which I replied, "I know and that's the problem!"

Enjoy your time at the finish and at the post-race reception. There's an amazing atmosphere and energy about the place with all those runners celebrating.

The downside of running in fancy dress is that it is slightly addictive. It now feels a little strange when I run a race in 'normal kit'. Whether you choose to do it again or to simply say, "I've done it and that's it!", you have something to be truly proud of. You'll have no doubt raised a heap of money for a great cause and had an amazing day out. The last 16 weeks training will all have been worth it – believe me! Your friends and family may have thought you were a little obsessed at times and they may never truly understand it, but once they see how much money you have raised and how many smiles you have brought to people, they will probably come round to your way of thinking…eventually!

There is nothing better than looking at your medal after
the race and thinking, "I did it!"

Total raised so far

£5,145.00

Believe it: in the end your efforts will pay off!

Top Tips – Post Race

36. Remember to Celebrate when you finish.
37. Enjoy the experience of the race – soak up the atmosphere.

10.1 The Post Race Review

With anything big in life it's always worth taking time post event to sit back and reflect on what you've achieved. I also find it good manners to thank all those people who supported me physically, mentally and of course financially!

For my first fancy dress London Marathon experience, I sent out a letter to all my donors, supportive friends and family; it still brings out a mixture of emotions reading it through now. I thought I would share it with you here to give you a feel for the day:

"Thank you! Thank You! Thank YOU!

On Sunday 22nd April 2018 I ran the hottest London Marathon Ever... dressed as a girl! Little Miss Sunshine to be Precise!

It was one of the most exciting races I have ever done. It was so hot. I carried an extra 2 litres of electrolyte in my backpack to keep me hydrated and drank most of it plus the extra litre that Claire gave me at 10 miles.

I hit 'the wall' at 17 miles, I then had to walk for a few minutes to get to the St John Ambulance man just to get some Vaseline for my sore shoulders. At 18 miles I saw Claire and the girls again and this gave me another boost to get me through the next few miles.

When I was next struggling, I found a pub! Literally a pub on the course serving BEER – so I stopped again and had a gorgeous half glass – it was the best energy drink ever. I quickly followed that by a couple of Salt and Vinegar crisps from a very kind, if not a little shocked, girl in the crowd!

Then it was on towards the finish. More high fives with the crowd and a bit more walking (especially in the shade of the tunnels). At Mile 25 I was interviewed briefly by Colin Jackson - I don't think it made it on to TV, but it was a great chance to talk!

And then came the final 1K - I've never known 1000 metres to take so long... I was almost shuffling at points, but yet again the crowd boosted me along. "Come on Phil, you can do it!". So, I did. 800, 600, 400 then only 385 yards to go... up the Mall to the finish.

Exhausted and feeling sick of energy drinks I crossed the line in 4 hours 25 Minutes.

The next 400m along the Mall to collect my bag was painful. I felt so sick. I had to stop and take the costume off - I'm sorry to all those people who stopped me to say congrats - I just couldn't talk!

BUT, I did it! and I've got the medal to prove it! Thank you ALL!

I am so grateful to all those who have donated to support my chosen charity this year – it is truly humbling to have raised so much. So, thank YOU!"

Finishing the world's greatest marathon, dressed as Little Miss Sunshine, in front of Buckingham Palace is an experience I will always remember!

A bit of history (this is a copy of the note I sent out with my race review)

"I haven't run the London marathon since 2010 so decided this year that I needed to do something a little different if I was to raise £2500 in 4 months.

My challenge, which many people have told me is totally mad, is to run the marathon dressed as 'Little Miss Sunshine'. Many people have already seen me out and about running around Thame, Long Crendon, Oxford and even Hyde Park – If you do see me please shout hello!

You can also donate by TEXT. Simply text RUNA96 to 70070 and the amount you want to donate e.g. RUNA96 £10 and send it to 70070

I have chosen to run for Children with Cancer UK having been moved to tears hearing the stories of the children and their parents and carers affected by cancer. When I read the posts of the other people running with me who have personally been impacted by cancer, I realise how lucky I am to be able to go out and run. If I can help others do the same one day then I know my four months training will have been worth it because it's nothing compared with what these young people are going through every day!"

Chapter 11. Breaking records

For some runners, it's enough to run the race in shorts and vest. For others, it's a big enough step up to do it in fancy dress, both for the thrill of just doing it and for the chance to raise more money. However, for some there's the lure of achieving something truly historic! If records are in your sights, then this chapter is for you. If not, then please skip this bit.

Once you have run in fancy dress and have a good idea that you can do it and survive, the next step in costumed running is to go for the big one, the ultimate goal, the crown jewel... a World Record!

Now, it's not for everyone. There is a lot to consider before you even get to the start line. It takes time, commitment, dedication and a massive amount of confidence.

Most of all, you will need to be extremely well organised. Entries for big races fill up fast and the timing for World Record attempts is something you will need clearance for from the start. If you miss the deadlines. you will not be allowed to enter that year.

When I planned my first Guinness World Record attempt, I wasn't organised! I half-heartedly read through the entry requirements, noted the entry deadline date and then left it to the last minute. Only to subsequently find there was a lot more I needed to get done in order for my entry to be officially recognised. In the end, my entry wasn't allowed that year, so I ran the London marathon in a costume just for fun. However, I was annoyed at myself for not reading up or being prepared; I enjoyed the race and learned a lot about proper fancy dress running, but I didn't get my record. To rub it in (and to spur me on), the lovely person removing the timing chip from my shoe at the end of the race, looked at me in costume and said: "If you are running for a record, you now need to head over there…" I looked across the finish area to see the man from Guinness World Records holding his clipboard with another record breaker and at that moment decided… "Next year, that will be me!"

11.1 Guinness World Record Application

The pinnacle of World Record attempts for the fancy dress runner has to be achieving a world-renowned Guinness World Record. The application process is straightforward if you are organised – you will need to get your entry in before the closing date. Details can be found at https://www.guinnessworldrecords.com.

Once you have registered, you will see your own dashboard. This outlines the record you are attempting, the target time and the stringent costume requirements. It's a lot of work, but all I can say is that it's worth it in the end.

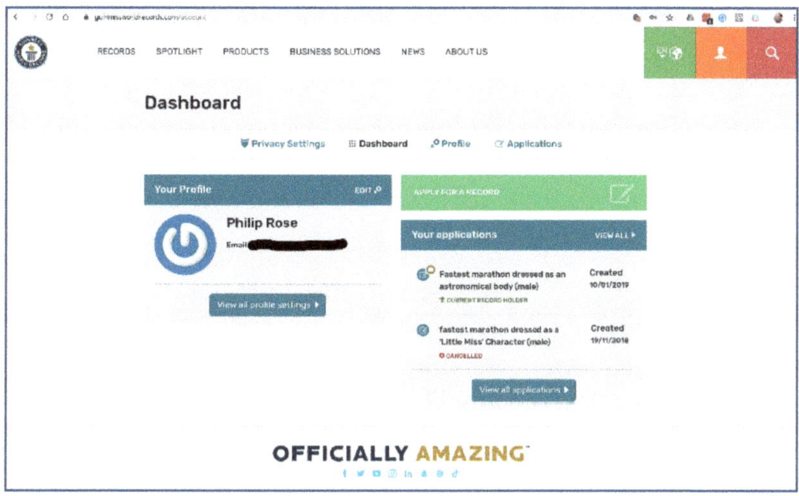

The process itself involves a number of specific steps that you need to follow:

(1)   Creating a suggested name for your record attempt;

(2)   Submitting photographs along with a written description of the costume, and;

(3)   Agreeing with the adjudicators that the costume meets their requirements.

Point 3 was the most difficult part for me as I had to create the costume from scratch, so was building it to meet the World Record requirements whilst also being mindful of my need to run in it. The whole process took me several months from start to finish. Most of that time was spent modifying and adjusting the costume to get it approved.

Most of that time was spent modifying and adjusting the costume to get it approved to ensure it met the Guinness World Record requirements AND was comfortable to run in.

Once the costume was approved online, I accepted that the costume would be subject to 'Adjudication on race day'. This meant that the costume had been approved in principle, but that final approval would be made on race day. So, I spent weeks training and raising money in the costume, whilst still, at the back of my head, thinking that it might not ultimately receive final approval!

To be honest, I actually became more anxious about the costume than the running. It became a bit of an obsession to get it right. Something inside drove me on, and on, and on… (and I am glad that it did!)

***TOP TIPS** – Achieving your Record*

40. Be persistent and confident in your determination to succeed in completing your chosen race.
41 If you are targeting a World Record, be sure to send your application in at least a month before the marathon entry deadline/ ballot date and to get your record application approved ahead of time – it takes longer than you imagine.

Over £6400 and a new Guinness World Record at the London Marathon 2019

Thank you to everyone who supported my Marathon attempt on April 28th. As reported across the media and in the April Edition of the Crendon Crier I was running my 5th London Marathon to raise money for Children with Cancer. To add to the fun of this amazing event I was also attempting a Guinness World Record as the Fastest Sun.

Your donations helped me raise over £6400 for this wonderful charity. I was lucky enough to carry two 'Beads of Courage' on my running shoe for the race. At every stage of cancer treatment, children receive a new Bead of Courage. The beads join together to form (often long) physical representations of their recovery, keeping a record of every hospital trip and treatment on their courageous journey. The beads I carried for the Marathon are to be sent to a child so she or he can remember the marathon as they undergo their treatment.

And to top it all I am pleased to say I am now the holder of a Guinness World Record for the Fastest Marathon dressed as a Sun completing the marathon, in costume, in 3 hours 52 minutes and 40 seconds! (and so, guess what's on my Christmas list this year… the 2020 edition!)

Once again thank you to everyone for your support.

Phil Rose

My final 'Thank you note' to my supporters!

Chapter 12. Your Notes

Use this page to record your thoughts, ideas and plans for your fancy dress marathon.

- Which marathon are you going to enter?

- What's the date of the race?

- Which charity do you want to run for?

- Why?

- What costume do you want to wear?

- Which training resources will you use?

- Which races will you enter as part of your training?

TOP TIPS – Achievement

42. Be Proud of your achievements - you are a star!

Chapter 13.   Additional "Bonus" Resources

I have included this section for those readers who want to see some examples of some of the letters I sent to raise awareness of my marathon plans (and so generate funding!)

13.1   Example Sponsorship Letter (as sent out in 2019)

Here's an example of a letter you can use to kick start your fund-raising campaign.

"Hello Again,

You probably know by now that I have been lucky enough to be selected to run the London Marathon again to raise money for Children with Cancer. They do an amazing job supporting both families and children with cancer. You can see my fundraising page here…

 https://uk.virginmoneygiving.com/PhilRoseVLM2019

You probably also guessed I'll be doing it dressed up again. and so now I can reveal my long slaved over costume... After all, why make it easy!

Last year was a very hot and SUNNY day - so I am hoping for a cooler day this year.

My Costume is now complete AND has been approved as an 'Official Guinness World Record' attempt at the Marathon Distance.

This year I will be running dressed as... The Sun! yes, the Sun!

I'm aiming to be the '**Fastest man dressed as the Sun running a marathon'**.

Training is going well - although as the mileage increases each week, I am feeling the strain! So far, I have managed a massive 5K in the costume – that means there are only another 37Km to go!

Why am I doing this?

I want to raise £2500 for Children with Cancer this year. And thought what better way to do it than dress up again.

So, I would love to have you as one of my sponsors… you can do it online here
https://uk.virginmoneygiving.com/PhilRoseVLM2019

Thank you for your support as always

Phil

13.2   Example Press Release to Announce your challenge

Bringing the Sun to London … Again…

Marathon Man Phil Rose is aiming to beat a Guinness World Record and raise money for Children with Cancer while running the London Marathon in April dressed as … the Sun!

22/3/19

Contact: Phil Rose on ███████████████████

Philip Rose is planning to do what many people consider unthinkable, and some even say downright silly. This year he is training to become the fastest "Sun" in London on April 28th. For that day he is running the London Marathon to raise money to support children with cancer in the UK and decided to do something a little different from the start. "I have run the London marathon four times previously," says Philip, a business coach from near Thame, Oxfordshire. "So, I decided this year I needed to do something far from ordinary if I was to raise over £2500."

"My challenge, which many people have told me is totally mad, is to run the marathon dressed as the Sun! I have applied to Guinness World Records to have my challenge monitored on the day, and, when successful, I will get become the fastest sun over 26 miles 385 yards!"

Philip ran the marathon last year, London's hottest ever, in a time of 4 hours 25 minutes. This year he wants to go even quicker if he is to achieve the Guinness World Record. To top the running achievement last year Philip raised over £10,000 for Children with Cancer.

Over the next two months you'll see Philip out running most days around the area 'disguised' in his 'handmade' Sun costume! If you do see him, please shout hello or honk your horn.

"I started my training in December and have been running three or four times per week since then," says Phil. "So far I have clocked up over 645KM and I've got another 6 weeks to go!"

"This will be my 7th marathon since 2008. I love running the London Marathon – the atmosphere is amazing. I love the crowds and the excitement of the event. I prepare for a marathon with a programme of training that starts out with around 16 weeks to go. I build up mileage each week and get long runs in each Sunday. This often means an early start, so I am back in time for family activities – it often means quieter Saturday nights too!"

Philip's mid-week training consists of interval training and recovery runs plus he goes circuit training on a Tuesday morning at 6:30am and Thursday evening. He also swims Monday morning and does a Pilates session Monday night – it sounds pretty intense and to be honest it is! (that's why I am so thankful to my wife and kids!) Preparing for running in my Sun costume adds another dimension to the training!

"I don't do every run, from the beginning of my training plan, dressed up. I start that once I have my 'base fitness' – this was in February this year. Before wearing the costume, I trained with the extra load in a rucksack which is about the same weight as the costume – although is a lot easier to run with. The other thing I must take into account is eating. Balancing the energy used in

training with the number of calories going in is pretty tough –
especially at first. I lost a couple of kilos in weight early on this year
as I 'forgot' to eat enough after my long runs. I now have increased
my calorie intake during the week after my runs and especially after
my long Sunday runs!"

To donate to this charity and support some wonderful people please
visit https://uk.virginmoneygiving.com/PhilRoseVLM2019

To help raise even more money Philip is offering local businesses
the opportunity to claim a promotional 'space' on the surface of the
Sun during his training – an ideal use of funds as we approach the
end of the tax year – please give him a call on ███████████ or
drop him an email to fastestsun@outlook.com

Editors' Notes

Contact details: Phil Rose

E: ██████████████████

T: ████████████

Children with Cancer UK's press office

E: media@childrenwithcancer.org.uk

T: 0207 404 0808

A little about Children with Cancer UK.
(https://www.childrenwithcancer.org.uk)

Chapter 14. About the Author

Phil Rose started running long before he can remember why he started running! At an early age however he only ever ran short distances, typically 100 and 200 metres. The thought of running the school cross country around Southampton Common filled him with dread!

Then over the years he realised the benefits of running for health, be it to keep him focused during University exams or running for fitness after work.

It was in 2007 that Phil sat down with his 5-year-old daughter to watch the London Marathon and his daughter asked him one simple question: "Could you do that daddy?"

There was only answer in Phil's mind – "Yes!" – and with that, Phil set about signing up for the Flora London Marathon 2008. He researched how to run a marathon and developed his own training plan based on that research. For that first marathon, Phil just wore running clothes and a wig. However, that was enough to kickstart the fancy dress 'thinking process'!

He then ran the London Marathon again in 2009, 2010 and Stratford-upon-Avon in 2011.

It wasn't until 2018 that he again came back to London for his first 'proper' fancy dress marathon, running as Little Miss Sunshine to raise money for Children with Cancer UK. The following year, in 2019, Phil chose to run for a Guinness World Record dressed as 'An Astronomical Body'. He is the current record holder with a time of 3 hours 52 minutes … and 40 seconds!

GuinnessWorldRecords ✓
@GWR

Here comes the sun ☀️ Philip Rose secured the record for the fastest marathon dressed as an astronomical body (male) today with a time of 3:52:40, while raising money for @CwC_UK #LondonMarathon 2019 #GetInspired

Finishing any race is an achievement that will make you smile and cry in equal measure. Doing it costume just adds to the emotion!

Whether you are a 'seasoned' fancy dress runner or new to the game I hope you have both enjoyed reading this book AND found it useful.

Good luck with your running. I hope one day to meet you and to hear of your journey and your successes.

If you would like further information, or have questions, please contact the author, Phil Rose, at
philip@fancyrunning.club